DOMAIN OF DEATH

DOMAIN OF THE DEAD

Copyright 2017© by Prism Thomas All rights Reserved

Published by :

G. Stempien Publishing Company
ISBN 978-0-930472-41-2

Bureau de la redaction: Nouveau quai, le pays, de Galles

Researchers :

Martin J.
Cohn Alain
M. Bodian

Edited by G.R. Stempien

English Introduction

Beneath the streets of Paris is an area of roughly 11,000 square meters which holds the remains of approximately 6 million dead Parisians. This location is known as the catacombs of Paris. The word catacomb from the Greek originally meant "hollow" but it has since come to mean something else. It came to mean a cavernous place under ground where bodies are buried.

The Parisian catacombs differ from those in Rome in several ways. One way is that they are the result of naturally formed quarries beneath the French city whereas the catacombs in Rome were created strictly for Christian burial. Another difference between the two systems of catacombs is that the last burials made in Rome were around 410 A.D. whereas internment did not begin in Paris until 1768. A third difference is that the burials in the Roman catacombs were an orderly process and the remains were properly interred whereas in the Paris catacombs the bones were tossed into place in a haphazard way.

Before 1768 all burials in Paris were above ground. When these graveyards turned into market places and locations of ill repute the public became enraged and clamored for a change. This eventually came in 1785 when bodies began emerging from one particular graveyard called the "Cemetery of the Innocents" due to various geological conditions and it was ordered by the state council that all burials from this cemetery be removed to the catacombs.

The removal of corpses and all of their attending inscriptions and crosses began on April 7, 1786. The process took fifteen months after which the "Cemetery of the Innocents" was destroyed and put to other uses. But this was only one, albeit huge, graveyard. Between the years

1787 to 1859 twenty-six more cemeteries were emptied of all burials and the bones and inscriptions were placed in the catacombs.

What follows is an exact verbatim description of what the catacombs looked like to a person who examined them post WWII. It is taken from an unpublished manuscript by Martin J. Cohn.

"One descends the ninety steps of winding, cold staircase into the perspiring halls of subterranean Paris. There, some sixty feet underground, begins the first section of the catacombs. The passageways are six to seven feet high, and three or four feet wide. Lining them on each side are small, dank, stone cubicles, which formerly served as dungeons. Some are provided with thick, splintered planks, which served as beds --- others did not have even this comfort.

"Beyond the dungeons is the section set aside as an ossuary. Here, the corridors become much wider, and on each side are shellacked bones and skulls, neatly stacked and interlaced in piles some six feet high and of varying depth - generally not less than five feet. The skulls are set into the walls of bones in fixed forms: some form crosses; the majority were geometrical designs. Occasionally, one also encounters pillars built up out of the carefully interlaced bones.

"The bones are grouped according to the cemetery from which they came, but other than this there is no way to divine the resting place of a particular individual. The bones of the renknowed(sic), such as Madam Pompadour, are interlaced with those of their servitors in the common community of death."

Inscribed upon plaques, pillars and tombs are the many inscriptions that deal with the fragility of life and the hopes of joy in the afterworld. Some are epitaphs over the original graves and others have simply been relocated from above ground to various locations below. The inscription are in five languages and some are from ancient times and these are mostly pagan and focus on death rather than spiritual beliefs. Many of the more "modern" inscriptions were selected for carving by L. Hericart de Thury who oversaw the transfer and removal of remains from above ground cemeteries during the first two decades of the 1800's.

NOTE ABOUT VISUAL QUALITY:

The researchers performed hundreds of hours of tedious work in the dark catacombs of Paris to produce this work. This was done in the 1940's. By their specific request the original documents - i.e. typed paperwork - is to be used in this publication so as to retain both the quality of their translations and a sense of the immensity of this project when it was undertaken. The editor of this publication as well as the publisher have adhered to their wishes, agreeing that the quality they wished to maintain would have been lost by "modernizing" the transcriptions. We apologize for any inconvenience this might have for the reader. Page 72 is only a partial.

G. R. Stempien

The work in the following pages is unique in that it accounts for all of the inscriptions found in the Paris catacombs. The inscriptions have been classified into three groups: the first - and largest - stresses the inevitability of death, the second concerns religious beliefs, and the third glorifies life.

HALT! THIS IS THE DOMAIN OF DEATH

Aequat omnes cinis: impares
Nascimur, pares morimur.
> Seneca.

La mort nous confond tous sous un même niveau;
La distance des rangs se perd dans le tombeau.

   Ashes equalize all:
   We are born unequal, we die equal.

Cf. James Shirley, <u>Cupid and Death</u>: "Death calls ye to the crowd of common men."

Cf. no. 51

Ainsi tout change, ainsi
tout passe; aussi nous-mêmes
nous passons, Helas! sans
laisser plus de trâce
que cette barque ou
glissons sur cette me ou
tout s'efface.

Lamartine

Thus all things change, thus all things
fly; we, we too, pass on and die, Alas!
leaving no more trace than this small
boat -- buoyed on a vast sea where all's
destroyed.

Ainsi tout passe sur la terre
Esprit, beauté, grâces, talent;
Telle est une fleur éphémère
Que renverse le moindre vent.

> Thus all expires on earth --
> Thought, beauty, talent, mirth;
> Like unto a fragile flower
> Which is upset by the least wind.

Cf. La Fontaine, The Florentine, Scene IX, ll. 159-160:
"Hélas, ce temps ne dura guère
Et ce ne fut pour nous qu'une fleur passagère."

Cf. nos. 2,22,60

Animae quibus altera fato Corpora
debentur Lethaei ad fluminis undam
Securos Latices et longa oblivia
potent.

Aeneid VI*

Ce sont les âmes à qui les Destins doivent un nouveau
corps, qui de long du Lethe, boivent l'onde qui
apaise et les longs oublis.

These are the souls to whom the Fates owe a new
body, the length of Lethe, drink the water which
appeases and the long forgetfulness. **

*Virgil, "Aeneid," Book VI, v. 713-715.
**The Lethean waters appease because they give
long forgetfulness. Grammatical figure of
"paratax."

Arrête! C'est ici l'empire de la mort.*

Halt! This is the domain of Death.

*Delille.

DOMAIN OF DEATH

Au banquet de la vie, infortuné convive,
J'apparus un jour et je meurs! Je meurs et, sur
ma tombe où lentement j'arrive, nul ne viendra
verser des pleurs!

*Gilbert

At life's banquet I was a wretched friend, I
appeared one day and heard no more jeers; I died
-- and none comes to shed his tears on my grave
wherein slowly I descend.

*Nicolas-Joseph-Laurent Gilbert, French poet who died
prematurely. The above verse which is carved on his
tomb, is taken from his poem, "Le Jugement Dernier."

Breves anni transeunt; et
semitam per quam non
revertar, ambulo.

Breves, les années passent, et je percours un sentier par lequel je ne reviendrai pas.

The short years go by, and I travel a path by which I shall not return.

Cf. Job XVI, 22: When a few years are come, then I shall go the way when I shall not return.

Cf. Ecclesiastes XII, 5 ...because man goeth to his long home, and the mourners go about the streets.

Combien de ceux qui étaient entrés
dans le monde avec toi en sont
déjà sortis? Leur vie a
été moissonnée comme des épis
dont les uns sont mûrs et les
austres verts.

Marc. Aurel.

How many of those who entered into the world with you have
already departed? Their lives have been reaped like stalks,
some of which are ripe, and others green.

Marcus Aurel: Thoughts: vi, 56: How many together with whom I
came into the world are already gone out of it.

vii, 40: life must be reaped like the ripe ears of
corn: one man is born; another dies.

...what is the difference between him who lives three days
and him who lives three generations?

Consummatum Est.

Tout est consomme

All is consumed

Crois-tu que la mort
soit loin de toi? Peut-
être en ce moment vole-t
-elle sur ta tête
et te menace-t-elle
du coup fatal?

Do you really believe that Death is
far from you? Perhaps at this very
moment she swoops down on your head
and threatens you with a fatal
blow.

Dans ces lieux souterrains, dans ces sombres abimes la mort confusement entasse ses victimes.*

In these underground places, these dismal deeps, Death, in confusion, her victims heaps.

Legouvé, "Poem of the Sepulchres."

Defecerunt sicut fumus dies mei
et ossa mea sicut cremium
aruerunt.*

Mes jours se sont dissipés comme la fumee, et mes os se sont consumés comme un bûcher.

My days vanish like smoke, and my bones are consumed like a pyre.

*Psalms, CII, 3.

Dispone domui qui a morieris et non vives

Dispose de tes beins parce que tu mourras, Et que tu ne peux toujours vivre.

Dispose of your goods because you will die: You cannot live forever

Esistenza del' Uom! Solo un instante infra il nulla e la tombs altro non sei. Allo spettacol fiero erran avante, Miserabil comparsa, arme e trofei; Fugge la tela, e appar cambiato il soglio, In erto si ma ruinoso scoglio.

Nott. Clement. I.5.

Existence de l'homme! Tu n'es rien qu'um instant entre le néant et la tombe! O miserable comprse, dans le spectacle altier les armes et les trophees venaient en tête; le rideau tombe, et le trône apparaît changé en un écueil encore debout, mais qui menace ruine.

Existence of man! You are naught but a single instant between nothingness and the tomb! O wretched supernumerary, arms and trophies played the leading role in the proud spectacle; the curtain falls, and the throne seems changed into rock still standing, but which is on the verge if dissolution.

15.

Esistenza del'Uom! Te breve
avversa Troppo ai desir la
cieca gente accus E a mille
obiette frivoli conversa
L'omaggio d'un pensier poi
ti ricusa, Ma vegetando coll
error a lato Muore al di
mille volte anzi suo fato.

Nott. Clement I.6.

Existence de l'homme! La foule aveugle t'accuse d'être,
par ta brièveté, trop contraire aux désirs. Et, adonnée
à mille objets frivoles, elle te refuse même l'hommage
d'une pensée. Mais végétant, l'erreur à ses côtés, elle
meurt chaque jour mille fois avant sa destinée.

Existence of a man! The blind crowd accuses you of being by
your brevity, too contrary to desire. And, given over to a
thousand frivolous matters, they refuse even the homage of
one thought. But vegetating, with error at their sides,
they die a thousand times each day before their destiny.

**Forme que de poussière humaine
quesoit le motif qui t' amène
ont ici foulé à chaque pas bris
monuments du trépas.***

Our ground is formed but of
human dust; think then,
whatever the trust that
brings you to these rooms
you trample death's wrecked
tombs.

* This is how the inscription appears in the Catacombs.
Apparently, however, the stone slab on which it was
carved was split off along the edge, since the original
inscription was undoubtedly the following verse of
Legouve:

Notre sol n'est forme que de poussiere humaine: Songe
donc, quel, soit le motif qui t'amene, que tes pieds vont
ici fouler a chaque pas un informe debris, monument du
trespas.

Haec lethi sedes; hic plurima mortis imago
ergo vide; maneat visum alta mente repostum.
Asoice reliquias fratrum, moriture viator cras tibi;
disce ergo vivere, disce mori. His pauper divesque
jacent, hic servus, herusque doctus et indoctus; cur
homo vane, tumes? Hos regit imperio mors; omnes
omnibus aequat, aspic dicque abiens: pulvis et umbra
sumus.

Hezette, vicaire de St. Jacques-du-Haut-pas.*

Voici le sejour de l'oubli; voici en grand nombre les images de la mort;
sois attentif, regards -- que la vision demeure gravee au fond de on coeur.
Considere les restes de tes freres, o passant qui dois mourir -- demain ce sera ton
tour: Apprends donc a vivre, apprends a mourir. Ici gisent le pauvre et le riche,
ici l'esclave et le maitre, le savant, etoir; l'ignorant. pourquoi, homme vaniteux,
te gonfles-tu d'orgueil? Sur ces hommesla mort exerce son pouvoir; elle les fait
tous egaux. Pense et dis en t'eloignant: nous ne sommes que poussiere et ombre.

Here is the abode of forgetfulness; here in great number are the images of death; be attentive, look closely -- that the sight may live engraved at the bottom of your heart. O wayfarer who must die, consider the remains of our brothers -- tomorrow it will be you turn: learn then to live; learn to die. Vain man, why do you puff youself up with pride? here lie the poor and the rich; here the slave and the master. the savant and the ignorant. Death exercises her power on these men -- she makes them all equal. In withdrawing from here, think and say, we are nothing but dust and shadow.

*This inscription, as well as many others in the Catacombs, were composed by Vicar Hezette of the Church of St. Jacques-du-Haut-pas. He apparently is unknown as a literary figure.

Heureux celui qui a toujours devant les yeux l'heure de
sa mort, et qui se dispose tous les jours a mourir.*

**Happy is the man who has the hour of his death always
before his eyes, and who daily prepares himself to die.**

Cf. Marcus Aurelius, Thoughts, II, 11:

Since it is possible that thou mayest depart from life this

very moment, regulate every act and thought accordingly.

Cf. Ecclesiasticus, VII, 36:

Whatsoever thou takest in hand, remember the end, and thou
shalt never do amiss.

Cf. nos. 34, 67, 71.

Hic in somno pacis requiesunt
majores.

Ici dans le sommeil de la paix, reposent les ancêtres.

Here rest our ancestors in the sleep of peace.

Homo sicut faenum dies ejus tanquam flos agri, sic efflorebit; quoniam spiritus pertransibit in illo et non subsistet; et non cognoscet amplius locum suum*

> L'homme! ses jours sont comme l'herbe; comme la fleur des champs il fleurit; qu'un souffle passe sur lui, il n'est plus et il ne connaît plus le lieu qu'il occupait.

> Man! his days are like grass; he blossoms as the flower of the fields; should a breeze pass over him, he is no more, and he no longer recognizes the place that he occupied.**

*Psalms, CIII, 15-16. The future tenses given in the Latin constitute an error on the Hebrew text, and should be translated by the present.

**The Hebrew text reads: "...and the place that he occupied does not recognize him." (M. Cohn)

Hucusque advenies, nec fas transire; tumentes
confringes fluctus hic, homo vane, tuos.

Hezette.

Tu viendras jusqu'ici et tu n'iras pas au dela;
Homme vain, tu brisera la tous tes flots gonfles.

You will come this far, and you will not go beyond;
vain man, here you will shatter all your swollen
waves.

Cf. no. 85

Ils furent ce que nous
sommes-- poussiere, jouet du
vent; fragiles comme des
hommes, faible comme le
neant.

-Lamartine

They were that which we
embrace -- by the winds
destroyed; fragile as the
human race, deficient as a
void.

Cf. nos. 2,3,60

in illo Tempore, ejicient ossa Regum et ossa principum ejus, et
ossa sacredotum, et ossa prophetarum, et ossa eorum qui
habitaverunt Jerusalem, de sepulchris suis! Expandent ea ad
solem et lunam et omnen militiam! Non colligentur et non
spelientur: in sterquilinium super faciem terrae erunt.*

En ce temps-la, on jettera les os de rois, et les os de ses princes,
et les os des petres, et les os des prophetes, et les os des habitants
de Jerusalem, hors de leurs sepulcres. Et on les etendra devant
le soleil, et devant la lune, et devant toute l'armee des cieux. Ils
ne seront point recueillis ni ensevelis, ils seront comme du fumier
sur la face de la terre.

> At that time, they shall throw out the bones of the kings and the bones
> of the princes, and the bones of the priests, and the bones of the prophets,
> and the bones of the inhabitants of Jerusalem, from their graves. And
> they shall spread them before the sun, and the moon, and all the host
> of heaven. They shall not be gathered, nor be buried: they shall be for
> dung upon the face of the earth.

Jeremiah, VIII, 1, 2.

Cf. II Kings IX, 37; Psalms LXXXII, 10; Jeremiah IX, 22

Insenses! nous parlons en maître,
nous qui, dans l'ocean des êtres,
nageons tristement confondus;
nous dont l'existence légère,
Pareille a l'ombre passagère,
commence paraît, et n'est plus.

Malfilatre*

Fools! Know you not we speak
as masters, we who, in this
sea of disasters, swim on,
sorrowfully confused. Our
frivolous crowd, like a
passing cloud, begins,
appears, and is diffused.

* Jacques-Charles-Louis Malfilatre (Malfillastre)
French Poet, 1762 - 1797.

Insensés que vous êtes, pourquoi vous promettez-vous de vivre
longtemps, vous qui ne pouvez compter sur un seul jour?*

Fools that you are, why do you assure yourselves of a long life?
You who cannot count upon a single day?

La même loi partout suivie
nous soumet tous au même
sort. Le premier moment
de la vie est le premier
pas vers la mort.

One law applies, inviolet -- we
all submit to the same fate. We
take the first step toward death,
the moment we first draw a breath.

La mort ne surprend point le sage;
Il est toujours prêt à partir,
S'étant su lui-même avertir
Du temps où l'on se doit résoudre à ce passage.
Ce temps, hélas, embrasse tous les temps:
Qu'on le partage en jours, en heures, en momens,
Il n'en est point qu'il ne comprenne
Dans le fatal tribut; tous sont de son domaine.
Et le premier instant où les enfans des rois
Ouvrent les yeux à la lumière,
Est celui qui vient quelquefois
Fermer pour toujours leur paupière.
Défendez-vous par la grandeur;
Alléguez la beauté, la vertu, la jeunesse;
La mort ravit tout sans pudeur;
Un jour le monde entier accroîtra sa richesse.

    La Fontaine.*

Death does not surprise the sage;

He is always ready to depart,

Having known to warn himself

Of the time when one must resolve upon this passage.

This time, alas, includes all time:

Even if one divides it into days, hours, moments,

There is no time which is not included

In the fatal tribute; all are of her domain.

And the first instant when the children of kings

Open their eyes to the light,

Is the one which sometimes comes

To close their eyelids forever.

Defend yourself by grandeur:

Cite beauty, virtue, youth --

Death shamelessly ravishes all;

One day the whole world will amplify her riches.

*La Fontaine, Fables, Bk. VIII, "La Mort et le mourant."
Cf. nos. 50, 74.

La mort nous frappés; craignez aussi ses coups: elle
est a vos côtes; mortels, preparez-vous.

Hezette.

Death has struck us; her blows you must fear;
mortals, prepare yourselves: she is near.

La tombe est un asile, et la mort un bienfait.

The tomb is a sanctuary, and death a benefit.

Roucher, "Printemps d'un Proscrit", ch. III.

Cf. nos. 32, 36, 46.

Lasciate speranza, voi ch'intricate.*

Abandonnez tout espoir, vous qui pénétrez dans ces lieux.

Abandon all hope, you who penetrate in these places.

*Dante, "Inferno" ch. III, Inscription on the gates of hell.

Le Trespas vient tout querir:
mais ne bougeons d'ou nous
sommes; Plutôt souffrir que
mourir; C'est la devise des
hommes.

La Fontaine*

Death comes to cure all: but
we rest where we lie; Rather
suffer than die; this is the
motto of men.

*La Fontaine, "Fables," Book I, Fable XVI, "La Mort et le bûcheron."

Cf. Sir Thomas Brown, "Religio Medici," pt. ii, 9: "We all labour against our own cure, for death is the cure of all diseases."

52.

Melius est mihi mori quam vivere.

Jon. 4,8

Il est quelquefois plus avantageux de mourir de vivre.

It is better for me to die than to live.

Cf. Jonah, IV, 3.
Cf. nos. 29,36,46.

Memento homo, quia pulvis es, et impulverem reverteris.*

Souviens-toi, homme que tu es poussière, et que tu retourneras en poussière.

Man, remember that you are dust, and that you will return to dust.

* Mass of the day of ashes.

Cf. GENESIS, III, 19; JOB XXXIV, 15
ECCLESIASTES III, 20 and XII, PSALMS,
CIV, 29.

Memento novissimorum noli oblivisci.

Souviens-toi de tes fins dernières; ne les oublie pas.

Remember your last ends; forget them not.

Cf. Ecclesiasticus, XXXVIII, 21

Memoriae majorum.

A la memoire des ancêtres.

To the memory of our ancestors.

Nihi...mori lucrum*

    phil. 1, 21.

Pour moi, la mort est un gain

For me, death is a gain.

*The complete text in Philippians 1, 21, reads, "For me to live in Christ and to die is gain." Such ommissions of text like the similar occur frequently in inscriptions in the catacombs and apparently were made deliberately in order to change the meaning. In every instance where there was an ommission or alteration of the original text, the resulting quotation which is presented is in less of a religious sense than the original

Mors te manet certissima: incerta sed
mortis dies. Ut mente semper excubes
Homoe latet lux ultima.

Hezette.

La mort t'attend, a coup ur. Mais incertain est le jour de
la mort. Pour que ton espirit soit toujours en l'oeil; ô
homme, ta derniere aurore reste cachée.

Death awaits you, unquestionably, but the day of death
is uncertain. So that your spirit may be always
watchful, o man, your last dawn remains hidden.

Mortel qui ne sait pas ce que vaut un instant, course
le demander a l'homme étendu sur son lit de mort.

Mortal who knows not the value of an instant, run, ask
it of the man stretched out on his death-bed.

Nisi granum mortuum fuerit, ipsum solum manet; Si autem mortuum fuerit, multum fructum affert.

John 12, 24-25.*

A moins que le grain de blé confié à la terre n'y meure, Il ne donne point de fruit; s'il meurt, il en produit beaucoup.

> Unless the grain dies, it rets alone;
> if it dies, it brings forth much fruit.

* Although the reference on the inscription is to both verses 24 and 25 of John XII, the quotation comes only from verse 24. (M. Cohn).

Cf, Revelation, II, 10.

Cf. no. 64.

Noctes atque dies patet atri janua ditis.*

    Les palais de la Mort nuit jour sont ouverts.**

    The door of Death's chamber is open night and day.

    *Virgil, "Aeneid," Book VI.

    **Delille

Οὐχ ὁσίη φθιμένοισιν

Non fas est mortuis
insultare.*

C'est une impiete due d'insulter aux
morts.

One should not insult the
dead.

*Homer, "Odyssey," XXII, v. 412.

Non metuit mortm qui scit contemnere vitam*

Il ne craint pas la mort, celui qui sait mepriser la vie

He who knows how to scorn life does not fear death

*Cato, "Distichs," Book IV, v. 22.

Nos jours sont un instant, C'est la feuille qui tombe.

Ducis.

Our days are but a moment, our
life -- a falling leaf.

...Nos ombres desolees desertent en pleurant leurs pompeux mausolees; Deux fois nous descendons dans la nuit des tombeaux!

Plus heureux ces mortels ignores du vulgaire, qui, sans être apercus, ont passé sur la terre! Leurs paisibles cercueils, respectes des mechans, N'éprouveront au moins que l'outrage des ans.

...Our grieved shadows tearfully desert their pompous mausoleums; twice we decend into the tombs' night!

More fortunate are those unaware mortals of the common herd, who unperceived, have passed over the earth! Their peaceful coffins, spared by the wicked, will meet only with the outrage of years.

Notre espirit n'est qu'un souffle, une ombre passagere, et le sorps qu'il anime, une cendre légère, dont la mort chaque jour prouve l'infirmite. Etouffes tôt ou tard dans ces bras invincibles, nous serons tous alors, cadavres insensibles, comme n'avant jamais été.

J.B. Rousseau.

Our spirit is naught but a breath, a transient shadow, and the body it enlivens, a buoyant ash, whose infirmity Death daily proves. Soon or late choked in those invincible arms, we shall all be thus, insensate cadavers, as though never having existed.

O mors! bonum est judicium tuum!

Eccl. 41, 3*

O mort! que ton jugement est remoli d' equite!

O Death! Your judgment is good!

* The reference given is to Ecclesiasticus, rather than Ecclesiastes.
Ecclesiasticus XLI, 2 "O, death, acceptable is thy sentence unto the needy."
(The discrepancy in verse reference is due merely to a difference in edition.)

Cf. nos.   29, 32, 36.

Omnem crede diem tibi diluxisse supremum.

Croyez que chaque jour est pour vous le dernier
Horace.

Believe that each day is for you the last.

48.

Optima quaeque dies miseris mortalibus aevi prima fugit; subeunt morbi, tristisque senectus: et labor, et durae rapit inclementia mortis.

Georg: Virgil, Lib. III, v. 66

La meilleure saison de la vie, pour les malheureux mortels fruit la premiere; puis s'savancent les maladies, et la vieillesse morose, et la souffrance; enfin la rigueur de l'inflexible mort (nous) saisit.

For unfortunate mortals, the best season of life is the first to vanish; then sickness, suffering and morose senility creep up on us; finally the rigor of unyielding death seizes us.

Parlate, orridi, avanzi: or che rimane dei ventati d'onor
gradi, e contrasti? Non son follie disuguaglianze umane?
Ove son tanti nuomi, a tanti fasti? E poiche andar del mortal
fango scarchi che distingue i pator dai gran monarchi?

Nott. Clement. I, 8.

Parles, restes hideux, parlez: que reste-t-il maintenant de ce qui
furent tant glorifiees, et de lurs exploits? Les inegalites humaines
ne sont-elles pas folies? Ou sont tant de noms et tant de fastes? Et
puisqu'ils seront liberes de la fange mortelle, qu'est-ce qui distingue
les patres des grands monarques?

Speak, hideous remains, speak out: what now remains of those who
were so glorified, and of their exploits? Are not human inequalities
mere foolishness? Where are so many names and so much pomp?
And since they will be freed from the mortal mire -- what distinguishes
shepherds from great monarchs?

cf. John Dryden, from the third book of Lucretius, "Against the Fear of Death:" "So many
monarchs with their mighty state, who ruled the world, were overruled by fate."

cf. James Shirley, "The Contention of Ajax and Ulysses," I, iii .

"The glories of our blood and state
are shadows, not substantial things;
there is no armour against fate;
sceptre and crown
must tumble down,
and in the dust be equal made
with the poor crooked scythe and spade."

cf. no. 1

Principium et finis: eternité.

Commencement et fin: eternité.

Beginning and end: eternity.

Protéger les tombeaux C'est honorer
les morts.

J. Delille.

To respect the tomb is to honor the dead.

Quelle est ta destinée, homme présomptueux? Ici bas ta durée éphémère et debile est plus fragile, helás! que la lampe d'argile, qui, dans ce gouffre obscur, t'éclaire de ses feux.

What is your destiny, presumptuous man? Down here your ephemeral and feeble span is more fragile, alas! than the lamp of clay, which, in this obscure abyss, lights up your way.

What presumption has man to count upon tomorrow? Where is it, this "tomorrow?" How many men will go to search for it beyond this world! Down here it is not certain for anyone.

This quotation is a probable adaptation from the "Imitation of Jesus Christ," Book I, chap. XXIII, v 1.

**Quels effroyables abîmes
s'entr'ouvrent autour de moil
quel déluge de victimes s'oofrent
à mes yeus pleins d'effroil!
Quelle épouvantable image De
morts, de sang, de carnage
Frappe mes regards tremblans!
Et quels glaives invisibles
percent de coups si terribles ces
corps pâles et sanglans?**

Jean-Baptiste Rousseau.

What dreadful depths half-disclose themselves around me! What a flood of victims confronts my dismayed eyes! what an appalling image of dead, of blood, of carnage strikes my trembling glances! And what invisible lances pierce these pale and bloody bodies, with such awful blows!

Quels enclos sont ouverts! Quelles étroites
places occupe entre ces murs la poussière des
races! C'est dans ces lieux d'oubli, C'est
parmi ces tombeaux que le temps et
la mort viennent croiser leurs faulx.
Que de morts entassés et pressés sous
la terre! Le nombre ici n'est rien, la
foule est solitaire.

Le Mierre

What sepulchres, what narrow places, are open!
The dust of races fills these rooms. It is among these
tombs, in those places of forgetfulness, that Time and
Death come to cross their scythes. Around them,
crowded and crushed dead are under the ground!
The number here is nothing; the crowd is solitary.

Qu'est-ce que chaque race! Une ombre après une ombre: nous vivons un moment sur des siècles sans nombre; Nos tristes souvenirs vont s'éteindre avec nous: Une autre vie, ô Temps, se dérobe à tes coups.

Le Mierre

>   What is each race! A shadow after a shadow; we live in a moment in Time's ceaseless ebb and flow; Our melancholy memories join us in death: Another life, Oh Time, has succumbed to your wrath.

Cf. nos. 2,3,22.

ane...
de la m...

What is death?
annihilation? Or, ... new
combination of the sa...

*This is an adaptation of Marcus Aurelius, "Thought

Quocumque ingrederis, sequitur mors, corporis umbra.*

Où que tu t'avances, la mort te suit, ombre du corps.

Wherever you go, death follows you, as the shadow follows the body.

*Cato, "Distichs," Book IV, v. 37.

Cf. no. 63.

Quocumque te vertas, mors in insidiis est.

De quelque côté que tu tournes, la mort est aux aguets.

No matter which way you turn, Death lies in wait.

Cf. no. 62.

Quod seminas non vivificatur, nisi prius moriatur.

> I Cor . 15, 36

Ce que l'on sème ne peut prendre vie que par la mort.

That which one sows cannot take life except through death.

Cf. no. 39

Quoeris quo jaceas post obitum loco? Quo non nata jacent.*

Vous voulez savoir où vous irez après la mort? Ce sera dans le séjour de ceux qui ne sont pas encore nés.

You wish to know where you will go after death? It will be to the abode of those who are not yet born.

*Seneca, "Troades," Act. II.

Relinquit dives omnia aliis et moritur.

Eccl. 11, 20*

A la mort on laisse tout.

The rich man has left all to others, and he dies.

*This is evidently a reference to "Ecclesiasticus" (verses 18 and 19 in most modern editions), rather than to Ecclesiastes.

Cf. "Ecclesiasticus" II, 18 and St. Luke XII, 19.

Cf. No. 13.

Si vous avez vu quelquefois mourir un homme, considérez toujours le même sort vous attend.*

If at some time you have seen a man die, always respect the fact that the same fate awaits you.

* Imitation of Jesus Christ, Book I, chap XXIII, v. 2.

Cf. nos. 17, 18, 34, 71

Sicut aqua effusus sum, et dispersa sunt omnia ossa mea.*

Je me suis répandu comme une onde, et tous mes os ont été dispersés.

Like water I was diffused, and all my bones have been scattered.

Cf. nos. 43, 69.

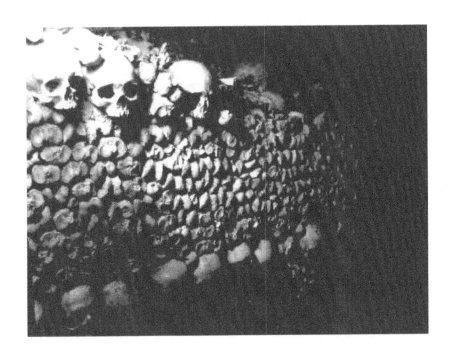

Sicut undra, dies nostri fluxerunt.

Comme l'onde, nos jours se sont ecoules

Like a wave, our days have flowed away.

Cf. nos. 12, 43, 68.

Silence, êtres mortels!*

Silence, mortal beings!

*This inscription appears on a plaque above the tomb of Gilbert.
See nos. 6, 79.

rXVXGGV

In all your actions, remember your inalterable end.

Cf. nos. 18, 34, 67.

Tel est donc de la mort l'inévitble empre; vertueux ou méchant, il faut que l'homme expire. La foule des humains est un faible troupeau, qu'effroyable pasteur, le temps mène au tombeau.

Legouvé.*

Such, then, is Death's inevitable reign; virtuous or evil each man must wane; the human throng is but a feeble flock, led by that dread pastor - Time - to the dock.

*Legouvé, "Le poèm de la Melancolie."

Cf. nos. 50, 77, 82, 98.

Tel qu'un flambeau qui se consume en s'allumant, nous commencons à mourir en naissant.*

    Like a candle which wastes away in being kindled, we begin to die in being born.

    *This is a possible adaptation from Marcus Aurelius, "Thoughts," vi, 15.

Cf. no. 26.

Tendimus huc omnes; metam
properamus ad unam omnia sub
leges mors vocat atra suas.
scilicet omne sacrum mors
importuna profanat omnibus
obscuras injicit illa manus.

Ovid.

C'est là que nous allons tous; nous hâtons vers cette unique fin;
la sombre mort appelle toutes choses sous ses lois. Oui, tout ce
qui est sacré, la mort cruelle le profane; sur tout, elle pose es mains
ténébreuses.

There it is that we are all going; we make haste toward that unique end;
sombre Death calls all things under her laws. Yes, cruel death profanes
everything that is sacred: she puts her tenebrous hands on all.

cf. no. 27.

75.

Tout naît, tout passe, tout arrive au
terme ignoré de son sort: a l'océan
l'onde plaintive, au vent la feuille
fugitive, L'aurore au soir, l'homme à
la mort.

Lamartine.

All is born, passes, arrives at the end, unconscious of
its fate: the fugitive leaf to the wind is mate;
to the sea -- the plaintive wave;
dawn to eve; man to the grave.

76.

Umbrarum his locus est; somni, noctisque soporae.

C'est ici le séjour des ombres, du sommeil et d'une nuit éternelle.

This is the place of shadows, of sleep and of restful night.

Cf. Algernon Charles Swinburne, "Hymn to Proserpine." After the proclamation in Rome of the Christian faith: "For there is no God found stronger than death; and death is a sleep." (M. Cohn).

Cf. no. 19.

Un monstre san raison, aussi bien que sans yeux, est
la divinité qu'on adore en ces lieux: on l'appell la
Mort, et son cruel empire s'étend également sur tout
ce qui respire.

Philip Habert*

The divinity worshipped in this domain is a monster with
neither sight nor mind; her name is Death, and her
cruel reign extends equally over all mankind.

*Philippe Habert, French poet who died in 1637. The above stanza is taken from "Le Temple de la Mort," a poem scarcely known today. (M. Cohn).

Cf. nos. 26, 50, 72, 83, 98.

Unusquisque in iniquatate sua morietur.

Jerem. 31, 30.

Chacun mourra dans son iniquité.

Each one will die in his sin.

Cf. II Chronicles, XV, 4; Numbers, XXVII, 3.

Ματαιοτη   ματαιοτης χπαντα ματαιοτησ *

Vanitas vanitatum, omnis vanitas.

Vanité des vanités, tout n'est que vanité.

Vanità delle vanità, è tutte le cose sono vanità.

Vanity of vanities, all is vanity.

*Ecclesiastes, I, 2 and XII, 10.

Venez gens du monde, venez dans ces demeures silencieuses, et votre âme, alors tranquille, sera frappee de la voix qui s'élève de leur intérieur: "C'est ici que le plus grand des Maîtres, le Tombeau, tient son école de vérité."

Tomb. de Hervey.

Come, people of the world -- come into these silent dwellings -- and your soul, once tranquil, will be wounded by the voice which rises from their interior: "It is here that the greatest of Masters - the Tomb -- conducts his school of truth."

82.

Vous avez vu tomber les plus illustres têtes,
Et vous pourriez encore, insensés que vous êtes,
Ignorer le tribut que l'on doit a la mort?
Non, non, tout doit franchir ce terrible passage
Le riche et l'indigent, l'imprudent et le sage,
Sujets à même loi, subissent même sort.

                                J. B. Rousseau.

You have seen fall the most illustrious of men,
And still, fools that you are, can it be that your ken
Is unaware of the homage we owe to Death?
Forget it not -- all must pass this dreadful Gate --
The rich, the poor, the fool, the sage, expires his breath
Subject to the same law; enduring the same fate.

Cf. nos. 26, 50, 72, 77, 98.

Beati qui moriuntur in Domino.*

Heureux, ceux qui meurent dans le Seigneur.

Blessed are those who die in the Lord.

*Revelation, XIV, 13: Blessed are the dead who die in the Lord.

Cf. nos. 100. 101, 109, 114

Canet tuba, et mortui resurgent.

I Cor. 15., 52.

Au son de la trompette les morts ressuciteront.

At the sount of the trumpet, the dead will come to life.

85.

C'est ici qu'il convient à l'homme d'être serieux, et de tenir son âme ouverte aux inspirations de la réligion. Puissé-je n'entrer jamais dans cette demeure sacrée qu'avec terreur et respect!

O Mort! que ton approche est terrible pour l'homme qui tourmenta sa vie de vaines inquiétudes de ce monde, et qui ne leva jamais les yeux vers le ciel.

Mortel, rachète le temps; mets à profit l'instant où tu respires; tu touches aux bords de l'éternité; tu vas bientôt devenir ce que sont ceux que tu contemples ici.

Le cercueil est la borne où s'arrêtent tous les desseins des hommes: ambition, tu peux aller jusque-là; mais tu ne passeras point au-delà.

> It is here that man should be serious, and open his soul to religious inspirations. May I never enter into this sacred dwelling but with terror and respect!
>
> O Death! how your approach is terrible for the man who tormented his life with the vain anxieties of this world, and who never raised his eyes toward heaven.
>
> Mortal, atone for time; profit by each breath you take; you are touching the borders of eternity; soon you will be in the same condition as those you now see.
>
> The coffin is the limit where all men's plans are stopped: ambition, you can go only thus far; but you will never pass beyond.

**Deposuit potentes de sede et
exaltavit humiles.**

St. Luke Ch. I*

Il a renversé les grands de leurs trônes et il a élevé les petits.

> **He has set down the mighty from their thrones and
> He has raised up the humble.**

*St. Luke, I, 52.

Cf. I Samuel, II, 8 and Job , 11.

Det illis Dominus invenire misericordiam
a Domino in illa die.*

Que le Seigneur leur accorde de recontrer la
misrericorde du Seigneur en ce jour-la!

May the Lord grant them to find mercy of the Lord in
that day!

* II Timothy, I, 18.

Deus mortem non facit.

Sap. I. 13.

   Dieu n'est pas l'auteur de la mort.

   God is not responsible for death.

Cf. no. 93.

Ecoutez Ossemens arides, ecoutez la
voix du Seigneur. Le Dieu puissant
de nos ancêstres, qui d'un souffle
créa les êtres, rejoindra vos noeuds
séparés. Vous reprendrez des chairs
nouvelles; la peau se formera sur
elles; Ossemens secs, vous revivrez.

Le France de Pompognan.

Harken, arid bones,
harken to the word of the Lord,
the powerful God of our fathers
will cause you to be restored.
New flesh will warm you;
skin will form; in one breath
He made all men. Dry bones!
You wil live again.

This inscription is a free translation of the latin in no. 112. It appeared in the Catacombs, however, as a separate inscription.

Eleemosyna a morte liberat.

Tob, 12, 9*

L'aumone delivre de la mort

Charity delivers one from death.

*****Tobit, XII, 9: for alms doth deliver from death.

Cf. no. 96.

Has ultra metas requiescunt beatam spem expectantes.*

Au-delà de ces bornes ils reposent en attendant une autre vie.

They rest beyond these confines, awaiting another life.

*This inscription was transferred to the Catacombs from its column in the old cemetery of the church of St. Sulplice. (M. Cohn).

Les âmes des justes sont dans la main de Dieu, et le tourment de la mort ne les touchers point.

The souls of the righteous are in the hand of God, and Death's torment will not reach them.

Cf. nos. 83, 101, 109, 114.

Lata porta et spaciosa via est quae ducit as perditionem.*

La porte large et le chemin spacieux mènent à la perdition.

Wide is the gate, and broad is the way, that leads to perdition.

*St. Matthew, VII, 13.

La morta ses rigueeurs a nulle autre pareilles;
on a beau la prier,
la cruelle qu'elle est se bouche les oreilles,
et nous laisse crier.

La pauvre en sa cabane, ou le chaume le couvre,
est sujet a ses lois;
et la garde qui veille aux barrieres de Louvre
n'en defend pas nos Rois.

De murmurer contre elle et perdre patience,
il est mal a propos;
vouloir ce que Dieu veut, est la seule science
qui nous me en repos.*

> Death has her rigors similar to no others; it is vain to pray to her, ruthless one that She is, She stops her ears, and lets us clamor.
>
> The poor man in his threshold cottage is subject to her laws; and the guard who watches at the gates of the Louvre does not defend our kings from her.
>
> To grumble against her and to lose patience is unseemly; to wish what God wishes is the only knowledge which puts us at rest.

La crainte de Dieu est le principe de la sagesse.*

Fear of God is the basis of wisdom.

*Job, XXVIII, 28.

Cf. Proverbs, I, 6-7; Ecclesiastes XII, 15.

Justicia liberabit a morte.

Prov., 10, 2; 11,4.

    La justice délivera de la mort.

    Righteousness will deliver one from death.

    Contrast Job, XII, 4.

    Cf. no. 90.

    Cf. Genesis, VII, 1.

Judici vivorum et mortuorum.

Au juge des vivants et des morts.

To the judge of the living and the dead.

Cf. Acts, X, 42

Jordens oro viker, för dem frid som
varar: grafven allt förliker; himlen
allt förklarar.

J. Wallin, Arch. d'Upsal.

Nos miseres expirent toutes
dans la paix qui ne finit pas,
la tombe, clot tous nos debates;
le ciel eclaire tous nos doubes.

        Our miseries evaporate in the peace which
        knows no rout; the tomb ends all debate,
        heaven answers doubt.

Intet lif Utan död;
ingen död Utan lif.

Le Prince Oscar de Suede. Visite du Mai 1867.

Toute vie a sa mort;
toute mort a sa vie.

        Each life has its death;
        each death has its life.

Invidia diaboli mors introivit in orbem.
Gen., ch. 3.

>C'est par la malice du démon que la mort es entrée dans le monde.

>The Devil's malice brought death into the world.

Although this inscription is attributed to Genesis (the reference is carved in the rock along with the quotation), the book contains

However, see Romans, v, 12.

Honneur, à Jehova, dont la toute-puissance, des corps ressuscités épurant la substance, Elève jusqu' à lui la faible humanité, et la revêt de gloire et d'immortalité.

Honor to Jehovah, whose omnipotence purifies the substance of raised bodies, raises feeble humanity unto him, and invests it with glory and immortality.

Treneuil, elegy on the tombs of St. Denis.

Memento Creatoris tui in diebus juventutis tuae antequamveniat tempus afflictionis.*

Souviens-toi de ton Créateur aux jours de ta jeunesse, avant que vienne le temps de l'affliction.

Remember your Creator in the days of your youth, before the time of affliction comes.

*Ecclesiastes, XII, 1.

Les yeux de Dieu sont fixés sur les justes et ses oreilles sont ouvertes à leurs prières.*

God's eyes are fixed upon the righteous, and His ears are open to their prayers.

*Psalms, XXXIV, 15.

Cf. nos. 83, 101, 109, 114.

Memento irae in die cosummationis.

Souviens-toi de la colére au jour de la consommation des siècles

Remember the wrath to come on the judgment day.

Cf. Ecclesiaticus, XVIII, 24.

Cf. no. 24.

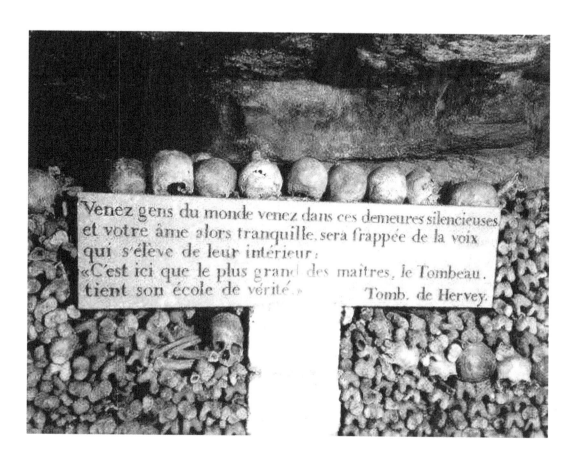

Memeto irae, quoniam non tardabit.*

Souviens-toi de la colere, car elle ne tardera pas.

Remember the wrath, for it will not tarry.

* Ecclesiaticus, VII, 16.

Cf., **Romans**, I, 18.

105.

Mors peccatorum pessima.

Ps. , 38, 22*

Elle est horrible, la mort du pécheur.

A sinner's death is the worst.

Mors sequitur vitam ; mortem altera vita sequetur,
vita beata bonis, aspera vita malis.

Hezette.

La mort suit la vie; une autre vie suivra la mort, vie bien heureuse pour les justes , cruella pour les méchants.

Death follows life; another life will follow death: A blessed life for the righteous, grievous for the wicked.

Mortuo homine impio nulla spes.

PROV. XI. *

Pour l'impie mort, il n'y a plus d'espoir.

For the impious dead, there is no longer hope.

*Proverbs, XI, 7.

cf. Proverbs, X, 28.

cf. no. 113.

Naturalis est separatis animae a corpore; spiritualis
est separatis Dei ab anima; que madamodum enim
anima est vita corporis, its deus est vita animae.

La séparation de l'âme et du corps est naturelle; ls séparation de Dieu
et de l'âme est spirituelle; et comme l'âme est la vie du corps, de même
Dieu est la vie de l'âme.

The separation of the soul and the body is natural; the separation
of God and the soul is spiritual; and as the soul is the life of the
body, God is the life of the soul.

Non tanget justos tormentum mortis.

Sap. 3, 1.

Les justes sont a l'abri des angoisses de la mort.

The torments of death will not touch the righteous.

Cf. Nos. 83, 100, 101, 114.

O Mort! est-il donc vrai que nos âmes heureuses n'ont rien à redouter de tes fureurs affreuses Et qu'au moment qui nous ravit l jour, tes victimes ne font que changer de séjour? Quoi! même après l'instant où tes ailes funebres m'auront enseveli dans tes noires tenebres, je vivrais! Doux espoir! Que j'aime à m'y livrer! De quelle ardeur celeste il vient de m'enivrer! *

O death! IS it then true that our fortunate souls have nothing to fear from your awful wrath? And at the cruel moment which robs us of day, your victims do nothing but change their abode? What! Even after the instant when your ominous wings will have shrouded me in your tenebrous darkness, I shall live! Sweet hope! How I love to believe in it! With what celestial ardor it intoxicates me!

* RACINE, Relig. c. II.

O poca oscura cenere, ti veggo, e mal cio che m'inspiri esprimer tento; io leggo in te dure vicende, io leggo I perigli d'un tardo pentimento; e mentre in te riguardo, e a te ripenso, m'appare il mundo un punto nell'immenso.

Nott. Clement I, 9.

Je te vois, ô peu de cendre obcure! Et vainement je tente d'esprimer ce que m'inspires; en toi je lis de dures vicissitudes, je lis les périls d'un repentir tardif; et, tandis qu'en toi je plonge mon regard, et qu'à toi je repense, le monde m'apparâit commeun point dans l'immensité.

O bit of obscure ash! I see you, and in vain I try to express what you inspire in me; I read in you hard vicissitudes, I read the perils of a late repentance. And, while I gaze at you and think of you, the world seems to ne a speck in infinity.

Ossa arida, audite verbum Domini...
Intromittam in vos spiritum, et vivetis.
Et dabo super vos nervos,
Et succrescere facias super vos carnes
Et super extendam in vobis cutem,
Et dabo vobis spiritum,
Et vivetis, ossa arida.*

        Os arides, entendez la parole du Seigneur...
        Je vais faire entrer l'esprit en vous, et vous vivrez.
        Et je mettrai des nerfs sur vous;
        Et je ferai croitre de la chair sur vous,
        Et j'etendrai de la peau par-dessus,
        Et je mettrai de l'esprit en vous,
        Et vous vivrez, os arides.

        Dry bones, hear the word of the Lord...
        I will cause breath to enter into you, and you will live.
        And I will lay sinews upon you, and will bring up flesh
        upon you, and cover you with skin, and put breath in you and
        you with live, dry bones.

*Ezekiel, XXXVII, 4-5-6.
cf. no. 89.

Post mortem corporis, non est locus poenitentiae.

Après la mort, il n'est plus temps de faire pénitence.

After death, it is too late to be penitent.

Cf. John Donne, "Divine Poems," Sonnet.

Cf. nos. 102, 107.

Pretiosa in conspectu Domini mors sanctorum ejus.

Ps. , 116, 15.

Elle est precieuse aux yeux du Seigneur, la mort de ses saints.

The death of His saints is precious in the sight of the Lord.

Cf. nos. 83, 100, 101, 109.

Qui dormiunt in terrae pulvere evigilabunt, alii in vitam aeternam et alii in opprobrium.*

Ceux qui dorment dans la poussiere terrestre, s'eveilleront un jour, les uns pour la vie eternelle, les autres pour l'opprobre.

Those who sleep in terrestrial dust will awake one day, some for life eternal, the others for opprobrium.

* Daniel, XII, 2.

cf. St. John V, 28-29.

...Quiconque boit de cette eau aura encore soif au lieu que celui qui boira de l'eau que je lui donnerai n'aura jamais soif.

Ev. Joanna IV*

Whosoever drinks of this water will still be thirsty, whereas he who drinks of the water that I shall give him will never be thirsty.

*St. John, IV, 13-14.

Sortez de la nuit éternelle; Rassemblez-vous, âmes des morts;
et, reprenant vos mêmes corps, paraissez devant Dieu; c'est
Dieu qui vous appelle.*

    Leave the eternal night's rim; gather you dead souls,
    without names; and, retrieving your mortal frames,
    appear before God, you are called by Him.

*Gilbert, "Le Jugement dernier."

118.

Stimulus autem mortis peccatum est.

I Corinth. 15, 56.

L'aiguillon de la mort, c'est le péché.

The sting of death is sin.

***Corinthians XV, 50.**

cf. Romans VII, 5.

Tumulus cum Aeternitate communicat.*

Le Tombeau communique avec l'Éternité.

The Tomb communicates with Eternity.

*St. Ephraem Syri, "Funereal Cantos."

Un cri religieux, le cri de la Nature, nous dit: "Pleurez,
priez sur cette sepulture; vos amis, vos parents dorment
dans ce sejour, monument venerable et de deuil et d'amour."

        A religious cry, the cry of nature, tells us: "Weep, pray on
        this sepulchre; your friends, your parents rest in this abode,
        venerable monument of the sorrow and of love.

*Delille, "Imagination."

Vidi impium superexaltatum et elevatum sicut cedros libani,
et transivi et ecce no erat et quoesivi eum et non inventus
est locus ejus.*

                Psaumes de David, Ch. XXXVI.**

J'ai vu l'impie adoré sur la terre:
Pareil au cèdre il cachait dans les cieux
Son front audacieux;
Il semblait à son gré gouverner le tonnerre,
Foulait aux pieds ses ennemis vaincus;
Je n'ai fait que passer, il n'était déjà plus.***

                Racine.

   * French translation of Latin:

   J'ai vu le méchant dans toute sa grandeur élevé comme
   les cèdres du Liban; j'ai passé et voici qu'il n'était
   plus; je l'ai cherché, et on n'a même pas trouvé
   l'endroit où il était.

   * English translation of Latin:

   I saw evil in all his grandeur raised up like the cedars
   of Lebanon; I passed, and behold! he was no more; I
   looked for him, and could not even find the place where
   he was.

** Psalms XXXVII, 35-36.

*** Racine's poem, which is carved in the rock directly beneath
the psalm, is an adaptation from the Latin, and not a
translation. The English translation of Racine's poem follows:

   I have seen the heathen worshipped on earth:

   Like the cedar he rose to the sky;

   His audacious brow called forth no mirth;

   The thunder seemed his will's ally;

   Crushed under foot the enemy corps:

   I merely passed -- and he was no more.

Chaque mortel paraît, disparaît sans retour, mais par d'illustres faits vivre dans le mémoire, voila la récompense et le droit de la gloire.

Each mortal appears, disappears without return, but by illustrious deeds alive in memory -- there is the reward and reason og glory.

The above is Delille's translation of Virgil's "Aeneid," Book X, v. 467, which appears as an inscription in the latin. (See no. 29) Delille's translation is inaccurate, but inasmuch as it appears in the Catacombs as a separate inscription, it is presented here.

Cur non et plenus vitae conviva recedes *

Sortz-donc de la vie, ainsi que d'un banquet **

Go out of life, then, as from a banquet.

Debilem facito manu, debilem pede coxo,
Tuber adstrue gibberum, lubricos quate dentes;
Vita dum superest, benest; hanc mihi, vel acuta
Si sedeam cruce, sustine.*

Qu'on me rende impotent,
Cul de jatte, goutteux, manchot, pourvu qu'en somme
Je vive, c'est assez: je suis plus que content.**

> Make me into a cripple, with a weak hand and a feeble foot; form me as a hunchback; shake my teeth until they rattle; all is well if my life remains: save it, I beg of you -- though I sit on a piercing cross.

* Verse of Mecenas, conserved by Seneca, <u>Letters</u>, 101.

Felix, qui potuit rerum cognosscere causas,
Atque metus omnes, et inexorabile fatum
Subjecit pedibus, strepitumque Acherontis avari!

                      Virgil - Georg. lib. 2.*

Heureux celui qui a pu apprendre les raisons des choses et qui a foulé aux pieds toutes les craintes, le Destin inexorable, et le bruit qu'on fait autour de l'Achéron jaloux.

Fortunate he who has been able to learn the reasons of things, and who has thrown underfoot all fears, inexorable Fate, and the noise made around jealous Acheron.

* Virgil, Georgicon, Book II, v. 490-492.

Ne timeas illam, quae vitae est ultima finis; qui mortem metuit, quod vivit, perdit idipsum*

Ne crains pas cette fin, qui est la fin dernière de la vie; celui qui craint la mort parco qu'il vit, cesse de vivre.

Fear not this end, which is the last end of life; he who fears death because he lives, ceases living.

*Cato, Distichs, Book I, v. 71.

cf. Martial, Epigrams, 47, Bk. X, line 13: Summum nec metuas diem, nec optes. (Neither fear nor wish for your last day."

cf. John Dryden, from the third book of Lucretius, "Against the Fear of death." This makes an hell on earth, and life a death.

Où est-elle la mort? Toujours future ou passée, a peine est-elle présente, que déjà elle n'est plus.

Where is Death? Always coming or past;

Scarcely is She present, then already She is no more.

Τί μοι' πόνων, τί μοι' ζιων
Τί μοι μελτί μεριμνω;
θνηθιν με δεῖ, χάν μη τέλω
Τί δε τον βίον πλανωμαι.

Anacréon.

"Imitation"

Pourquoi tous ces regrets, cette peine infinie? Pourquoi sur notre sort et pleurer et gémir? Puisqu'il faut tôt ou tard malgré nos soins mourir; amis, ne troubons point le rêve de la vie.

Why all these regrets, this endless strife? Why shed tears and groan over our fate? despite our pains, we die soon or late; friends, do not disturb the dream of life.

Stat sua cui qui dies:

>
> Breve et irreparabile tempus
> Omnibus est vita;
> Sed faman extendere factis,
> Hoc virtutis opus.
>
>   Aeneid lib. X, v. 467.

    La duree de la vie est fixee pour chaque homme; et pour tous les hommes, elle un temps bref et irreparable; mais etendre sa renomee par de hauts faits, c'est l'ouvrage de la vertu.

    Life's span is fixed for each man; and for all men, it is a brief and irreparable time; but to exgtend one's fame by worthy deeds is the work of virtue.

Appendix II

1. Ossements du cimetière des Innocents, déposés en avril 1786.

2. Ossements du cimetière des Innocents, déposés en avril 1787.

3. Ossements du cimetière de St.-Etienne-des-Grès, déposés en mai 1787.

4. Ossements du cimetière de St. Eustache, déposés en mai 1787.

5. Ossements du cimetière des Innocents, déposés en 8bre 1787.*

6. Ossements du cimetière des Innocents, déposés en janvier 1788.

7. Ossements du cimetière de St. Landri, le 18 juin 1792.

8. Ossements du cimetière de Saint-Julien-des-Ménétriers, le 18 juin 1792.

9. Ossements de l'église Ste Croix-de-la-Bretonnerie, le 20 octobre 1793.

10. Ossements de l'église des Bernardines du 12 décembre 1793.

11. Ossements de l'église de St. André-des-Arts, le 24 février 1794.

12. Ossements du cimetière et de l'église St. Jean de l'Hôtel de Ville, le 4 janvier 1804.

13. Ossements de l'église et du cloître des Capucins-St Honoré, le 28 mars 1804.

14. Ossements de l'église et du cloître des Capucins-St.-Honoré, le 29 mars 1804.

* "8bre," early notation for "octobre."

II - 2.

15. Ossements de l'église et du cloître des Blancs-Manteaux, le 22 juin 1804.

16. Ossements de l'église et du cloître du Petit St. Antoine, le 17 juillet 1804.

17. Ossements du cimetière St. Nicolas-des-Champs, le 21 août 1804.

18. Ossements du cimetière St. Nicolas-des-Champs, le 24 août 1804.

19. Ossements du cimetière de St. Laurent, déposés en 7bre 1804.*

20. Ossements du cimetière de St. Esprit,** déposés le 7 novembre 1804.

21. Ossements du cimetière de St. Laurent, déposés le 7 novembre 1804.

22. Ossements du cimetière de St. Laurent, le 7 novembre 1804.

23. Ossements du cimetière des Innocents, déposés le 2 juillet 1809.

24. Ossements du petit cimetière de l'Isle-Saint-Louis, le 26 septembre 1811.

25. Ossements de l'hôpital de la Trinité, rues St. Denis et Greneta, le 6 janvier 1814.

26. Ossements de l'hôpital de la Trinité, rues St. Denis et Greneta, le 25 janvier 1814.

27. Ossements du couvent des Carmes de la Place Maubert, déposés le 25 janvier 1814.

28. Ossements de l'église et du cloître Saint Benoit, déposés les 13 et 14 février 1817.

* "7bre," early notation for "septembre."
** St. Esprit-en-Greve

II - 3.

29. Ossements du cimetière de Vaugirard (élargissement du boulevard exterieur), déposés en 1838 dans l'ossuaire de l'ouest et transférés dans les Catacombes en 7bre 1859.

30. Ossements de l'ancien cimetière St. Nicolas-des-Champs, déposés de 1843 a 1846 dans l'ossuaire de l'ouest et transférés dans les Catacombes en 7bre 1859.

31. Ossements de l'ancien cimetière de la Magdeleine (rue de la Ville l'Evêque nos. 1 et 2), déposés en 1844 dans l'ossuaire de l'ouest et transférés dans les Catacombes en septembre 1859.

32. Ossements de l'ancien cimetière St. Jean (rue du Faubourg Montmartre no. 60), déposés en 1846-1847 dans l'ossuaire de l'ouest et transférés dans les Catacombes en 7bre 1859.

33. Ossements de l'ancien cimetière St. Laurent, déposés en 1848 dans l'ossuaire de l'ouest et transférés en 7bre 1859.

34. Ossements de l'ancien cimetière St. Jacques-du-Haut-Pas, déposés en 1850 dans l'ossuaire de l'ouest et transférés en 7bre 1859.

35. Ossements de l'ancien cimetière attenant à la Tour St. Jacques-la-Boucherie, déposés en 1852 dans l'ossuaire de l'ouest et transférés dans les Catacombes en 7bre 1859.

36. Ossements recueillis rue de Douai no. 5, emplacement d'une ancienne léproserie, déposés en 1858 dans l'ossuaire de l'ouest et transférés dans les Catacombes en septembre 1859.

II - 4.

37. Ossements recueillis sous le pavé de l'église St. Nicolas-des-Champs, déposés en 1859 dans l'ossuaire de l'ouest et transférés dans les Catacombes en 7bre 1859.

38. Ossements des anciens cimetières de la Trinité et de St. Leu, Boulevard Sébastopol, déposés en 1859 dans l'ossuaire de l'ouest et transférés dans les Catacombes en 7bre.1859.

39. D.M. Ossements, l'église de St. Laurent, déposés le 17 avril MDCCCLXXI.

INTRODUCTION

1. Catacombes établies par ordre de Mr. Thiroux de Crosne, Lt. Général de Police, par les soins de Mr. Charles Axel Guillaumot, Inspecteur Général des Carrières, en MDCCLXXXVI. Restaurées et augmentées par ordre de Mr. le Comte Frochot, Conseiller d'état Préfecture du Département de la Seine, par Mr. Héricart de Thury, Ingénieur en Chef des Mines, Inspecteur Général des Carrières, MDCCCX.

> Catacombs established by the order of Mr. Thiroux de Crosne, Lt. General of Police, through the interest of Mr. Charles Axel Guillaummont, Inspector-General of quarries in 1786. Restored and enlarged by the order of Count Frochot, Councillor of State from the department of the Seine, through Mr. Héricart de Thury, Chief Engineer of Mines and Inspector-General of Quarries, 1810.

2. Collection minéralogique des carrières de la plaine de Montrouge et des Catacombes, 1811: échantillons des bancs de pierre de cette carrière (hauteur totale de 66.50); fragment de l'aqueduc d'Arcueil, construit par les Romains au-dessus de cette carrière pour mener les eaux de Rungis au Palais des Thermes de l'empereur Julien; échantillons des bancs de terre depuis la surface du sol jusqu'au banc de roche (hauteur totale de 12.50).

> Mineralogical collection from the quarries of Montrouge plain and the Catacombs, 1811: samples of layers of stone of this quarry (total height - 66 meters, 50 centimeters); fragment from the Arcueil acqueduct, constructed above this quarry by the Romans, to carry the waters of Rungis to the Palace of Thermes of the emperor Julian; samples of layers of earth from the surface of the ground down to the layers of rock (total height - 12 meters, 50 centimeters).

I - 2.

3. D.M. Combats de la Place de Grève de l'Hôtel de Brienne et de la rue Meslée, les 28 et 29 août 1788.

    Battles of Grève Square of the Hotel Brienne 2nd of august of Meslee St., 28 and 29, 1788.

4. D.M. Combat a la manufacture de Reveillon, Faubourg St. Antoine, le 28 avril 1789.

    Battle of the Reveillon factory, Faubourg St. Antoine, April 28, 1789.

5. D.M. Combat au Château des Tuileries, le 10 août 1792.

    Battle of the Chateau of the Tuileries, August 10, 1792.

6. Crypte de la Sépulture des Victimes des 2 et 3 septembre 1792.
D. O. M. Piis Manibus. Civium diebus II et III Septembris anno Domini MDCCXCII. Lutetiae trucidatorum.
Hic palmam expectant cives virtutis amore conspicui; cives patriae, legumque Deique cultores, diris heu! tempestatibus acti, immoti tamen, ut scopuli, rectique tenaces, supremae plebis deliramenta perosi. Hos, dum crudelis discordia sceptra tenebat hortatrix scelerum, contemptaque jura jacebant, saeva caede cohors furiis incensa peremit. Siste gradum, inque pios fletus erumpe, viator, castas funde preces et candida lilia sparge. Lux perpetua luceat eis.   Hezette.

    Aux mânes sacrés des citoyens massacrés à Paris le 2 et le 3 septembre en l'an de Dieu 1792.

I - 3.

Ici attendent la palme les citoyens remarquables par leur amour de la vertu, respectueux des lois, adorateurs de Dieu. Ils furent emportés, hélas, par de cruelles tempetes. Cependant inébranlables comme des rocs, justes, fermes ils ont haï les extravagances de la plèbe toute puissante. Alors que la cruelle discorde tenait le sceptre (en mains) - elle qui pousse aux crimes -- et que les lois étaient à terre, méprisées, une troupe brûlante de fureur les a fait périr d'une mort cruelle. Arrête tes pas et verse des larmes sur ces hommes justes, passant, répand de saintes prières, dépose des lys blancs. Que la lumiere éternelle les illumine.

Crypt of the victims of September 2 and 3, 1792. To the sacred shades of the citizens massacred at Paris on September 2 and 3 in the year of our Lord, 1792.

Here those law-abiding citizens, distinguished by their love of virtue and of God, await their award. Alas, they were carried away by raging tempests. However, resolute as rocks, and righteous, they hated the extravagances of the omnipotent mob. When cruel dissension - she who incites men to crime - took the sceptre in hand, and when the laws were trampled upon and scorned, a crowd inflamed with fury caused them to perish. Halt, passer-by, and shed your tears on these righteous men. Recite holy prayers, and adorn their grave with white lilies. May the eternal light cast its rays on them.

7. A la mémoire de Françoise Gellain, Dame Legros: Couronnée par l'académie française, en 1784, décédés à Paris le 12 X^{br}, 1821, agée de 75 ans. Son époux, ses enfants, sa famille, ses amis.

Ici repose en paix cette femme admirable,
Qui de Latude*enfin fit ouvrir les cachots.
Trente-deux ans de fer, O femme incomparable,
Excitent ta pitié! Pour toi plus de repos;
Après trois ans et plus, par ta persévérance,
Tu sus l'en arracher; l'Europe t'admira.
Le prix de la vertu couronna ta constance,
Et la postérité jamais ne t'oubliera.

>To the memory of Francoise Gellain, Lady Legros: crowned by the French Academy in 1784, died in Paris December 12, 1821, aged 75 years. Her husband, her children, her family her friends.
>
>Here rests in peace that admirable woman, who finally caused the dungeons to be opened for de Latude. Oh incomparable woman, thirty-two years in irons excite your pity! For you, no more rest; after three years and more, by your perseverance, ... will admire you. Virtue's award will crown your constancy, and posterity will never forget you.

* Jean-Henri de Latude was an adventurer born at Montagnac in 1725. Following intrigues against Madame Pompadour, he was enprisoned in turn in the Bastille, Vincennes, Châtelet, and Charenton. He escaped several times, but was re-captured, and remained a prisoner for thirty-five years, until Francoise Gellain caused him to be released. He died in 1805.

I - 5.

8. Jacques de Bordeaux, Sr. de Saint-Aubin-Sur-Yonne, Conseiller du Roy au Parlement, épousa demoiselle Madeleine Sauvat. Mort en 1593. David & Jesus.*

    Jacques de Bordeaux, Lord of Saint-Aubin-on-the-Yonne, Counselor of the king to Parliament, Miss Madeleine Sauvat. Died in 1593. David and Jesus.

* This inscription was on a copper plate, attached to a stone cross, in the section of the Catacombs containing the remains from the Trinity cemetery. This plaque, which came from one of the tombs in that cemtery, is no longer in the Catacombs, having disappeared in 1902.

9. Coeur du Général de Division, Baron Campi. 1894.**

    Heart of Baron Campi, General of the Division. 1894.

** The General's heart was found on June 28, 1893, in an excavation at Niel Avenue, and sent to the Catacombs. It was enclosed in a lead box, itself formed in the shape of a heart, with a parchment bearing the following inscription: "Coeur du Général du Division, Baron Campi, mort à Lyon, le 14 octobre 1832. Embaumé par Mr. Jourdan, pharmacien." (Heart of Baron Campi, General of the Division, died at Lyon, October 14, 1832. Embalmed by Mr. Jourdan, pharmacist.) After having been opened, the heart was replaced in the box, and placed in a special receptacle in the Catacombs on May 9, 1894.

I - 6.

10. Cet ouvrage fut commencé en 1777, par Décure, dit Beauséjour, vétéran de Sa Majesté, et fut fini en 1782.

    This work was begun in 1777 by Décure, called Beauséjour ("good sojourn"), veteran of His Majesty, and was finished in 1782.

11. Port-Mahon.* Sculpté par Décure, carrier (1777-1782). Restauré en 1937 par les ouvriers de l'inspection générale des carrières sous la direction de M. Roger Eugène, sculpteur agent de cette inspection générale.

    Port-Mahon. Sculpted by Decure, miner (1777-1782). Restored in 1937 by the workers of the General Inspection of Quarries, under the direction of Mr. Roger Eugène, sculptor agent of that Inspection.

* The fortress of Port-Mahon, principal city of the Balearic Islands. One of the workers in the Catacombs, formerly a prisoner in Port-Mahon, spent his free time for five years sculpturing in the rock of the Catacombs a reproduction of that fortress. He was killed by a cave-in in 1782, in attempting to construct a stairway to provide a better view of his just-finished work.

12. Porte Roche. 1866.
    Rock doorway.

13. Puits.
    Well.

14. Tombe Issoire.
    Issoire Tomb.

15. Le sol de cette fontaine est de 48 m. 4 au-dessus de la mer (146 pieds 9.6).*
    The soil of this spring is 48 meters, 4 centimeters above sea-level (146 feet, 9.6 inches).

* Actually, the proper conversion of the metric figure would result in 157 feet, 6.85 inches.

16. Le sol de cette fontaine est de 15 mètres 4 au-dessus du zéro du Pont de la Tournelle (46 pieds 3.6).**
    The soil of this spring is 15 meters, 4 centimeters above the zero-reckoning of Tournelle Bridge (46 feet, 3.6 inches).

** Actually, the proper conversion of the metric figure would result in 49 feet, 3.96 inches.

17. Cloche de Fontis Hauteur 11 m. 00. D. 1874.

18. Cloche de fontis.*** Hauteur 11 m. 35. D. 1875.

19. Cloche de fontis.*** Hauteur 10 m. 20. D. 1875.

*** A "cloche de fontis" is a large, bell-shaped hollow in the corridor ceiling, formed by the giving-way of the rock.

20. Profondeur 54 pieds. 17 metres 53.****
    Depth, 54 feet. 17 meters, 53 centimeters.

**** This notice was found at the exit, at the foot of the stairway. The proper conversion of the metric figure would result in 57 feet, 5.79 inches.

FINI

Made in the USA
Las Vegas, NV
18 May 2025